THE
L A S T
GENERATION
O F
TRUTH

D1714155

THE
LAST
GENERATION
OF
TRUTH

Daniel L. Butler

The Last Generation of Truth

by Daniel L. Butler

©1989 Word Aflame Press
  Hazelwood, MO 63042-2299

ISBN 0-932581-58-7

Cover Design by Tim Agnew

All Scripture quotations in this book are from the King James Version of the Bible unless otherwise identified.

Printed in United States of America

Printed by

*To our cherished son
Dane,
who is being raised as a
fourth-generation Oneness Pentecostal*

Contents

Foreword

This book is indeed a very special research into ecclesiastical history as well as an astute observation of the development and deterioration of denominational Christianty.

Dan Butler has brought to the attention of us all the necessity of maintaining a third and fourth generation of Pentecostal commitment and sacrifice equal to the first generation of Pentecostals. This dedication is needed to preserve revival in our midst, for none of us want stagnation and institutionalism to destroy revival fires. It is vitally important that we look into what is needed to maintain the gushing flow of revival. We do not want to leave behind us a despicable era in history of compromising, spineless preaching that, because of the pressure of the times, watered down the great truths of doctrine that we hold dear.

This book will set your thinking faculties spinning into the right direction. Read it over a couple of times to get the full gist of Brother Butler's well-said statements as well as his timely research. Thank you, Brother Butler, for being willing to put into writing the sober things we need to think about and reflect upon. This book will help us to see ourselves in the light of the past and the need

of the present as well as illuminate the heritage
we pass on to the future.

Nathaniel A. Urshan
General Superintendent
United Pentecostal Church International

10

Preface

Several years ago, while working with young people of the United Pentecostal Church International, I witnessed some trends that caused much concern. A tendency for self-centeredness in third-generation Pentecostals triggered apprehension and anxiety about what had provoked, and what would be the outcome, of the trends. In prayer, the Lord gave me understanding regarding the evolution of self-centered tendencies and the expected outcome if the trends continued unchallenged. I was able to translate the tendencies into first-, second-, and third-generation characteristics that naturally develop out of organizational development, expansion, plateau, and decline.

Historical chronicles demonstrate the potential for the United Pentecostal Church International to experience growth, plateau, and decline. Many movements across the pages of history have followed such cyclic tendencies. In astonishment, I discovered the historical significance of the sectarian cycle and considered its application to the Oneness movement today.

In prayer and devotion, I developed the concepts shared in this book. My desire is for those who read this book to allow fresh consecration and commitment to be etched deep in their souls, promulgating prayer and revival dynamics in our generation.

Acknowledgements

Although the list of individuals who helped contribute to the ultimate development of this book is inexhaustible, several outstanding individuals deserve recognition. In tones of deep love, thank you, Pam, my cherished wife, for granting encouragement, support, and love while living a devoted life to God. To my parents, thank you for the Pentecostal home, the Christian atmosphere, the God-centered lives you lived, and all the prayers. To my pastor and dear friend, thank you, Brother Urshan, for faithfully serving the flock in Indianapolis, teaching, preaching, and guiding me in the ways of God.

To my dear friend and associate Brother Jack DeHart, thank you for taking me as your Timothy and training me in the ministry. Thank you, United Pentecostal Church International, for your fellowship, support, and giving me space to minister. Especially, thank you, Jesus, for continually shepherding my soul.

1

The Sectarian Cycle

As the crises of state independence and slavery were tediously settled by the Civil War, a similar battle was being fought at the Methodist Episcopal Church South general convention. The topic of discussion on the floor was whether or not ladies should wear lace on their bonnets. Though it may seem extreme to us today, the outcome of the discussion was a banning of lace on ladies' bonnets because it was unnecessary and pointed toward extravagant living. This and many similar practices were categorized as "superfluity of naughtiness." The Holiness movement was vibrant and alive!

Less than one hundred years later, in a similar Methodist general convention, the topic on the discussion floor was whether or not to allow dancing on Methodist church premises. Social drinking and smoking had already been condoned, and the stand against dancing in the church was the only thread remaining from the practical holiness teachings of the early Methodism of John Wesley and of the later Holiness movement. On the basis that church people would attend dances anyway and that it was better to prevent the people from being hypocritical, the convention decided to allow dancing in the church house. Within three generations of its spiritual zenith in America, most major holiness teachings had slipped away from the Methodist church.[1]

Today the United Methodist Church has little in common with the movement that John Wesley established in the 1700s or with the Methodists of the 1800s. Fervent devotion, evangelistic zeal, holiness emphasis, conservative theology, and growth that characterized the movement three generations ago are gone. As a Methodist bishop recently noted, "Now we are tired, listless, fueled only by the nostalgia of former days, walking with a droop, eyes on the ground, discouraged, putting one foot ahead of the other like a tired old man who remembers, but who can no longer perform."[2]

This stunning reversal illustrates a common phenomenon in the history of religious movements that has been called the sectarian cycle. (The word *sectarian* is not used here in a pejorative way, but simply to refer to a religious group.) This historical pattern has significant implications for the Oneness Pentecostal movement today.

The sectarian cycle refers to frequently re-occurring trends in the life of various religious movements and denominations; often, the third generation of such a group is the last one to embrace the full array of truth for which the movement stands. In other words, the third generation of a religious organization is often the last generation of truth.

The trend is for the first generation to grow, the second to reach a peak, and the third to experience decline. Because of intellectualism and rationalization, the third generation often rejects divine truths, and consequently God turns to people who are open to and hungry for the move of His Spirit.

Much of the United Pentecostal Church is comprised of third-generation believers, and within a couple of decades, the leadership of the United Pentecostal Church is likely to be composed predominantly of third-generation believers. Consequently, the Oneness Pentecostal movement stands at a threshold of decision. If the United Pentecostal Church is to reverse the trend of history and escape the sectarian cycle, the third generation of the Oneness Pentecostal movement must aggressively fight the tendency to decline.

The third generation of believers must find an original, first-generation experience in God if it is to avoid being the last generation of truth.

In approximately a hundred years, Israel crossed the Red Sea, passed through the wilderness, entered the Promised Land, inhabited the Abrahamic inheritance, and then lost contact with God. The Lord had graciously granted Joshua health and years (110 total) to serve as a great leader, and he judged Israel into its third generation from the Red Sea experience. However, when Joshua died "and also all that generation were gathered unto their fathers: . . . there arose another generation after them, which knew not the LORD, nor yet the works which he had done for Israel" (Judges 2:10). The third generation became the last generation of truth, and the fourth generation arose not knowing God. Moses represented the first generation; Joshua, the second; the descendants judged by Joshua, the third; and the generation after them who did not know God, the fourth.

Saul, the first monarch of Israel, ruled for forty years, and despite his ultimate downfall, he led the nation into stability and growth. King David, considered to this day by Jews as the greatest king in the history of the nation, reigned over Israel through times of spiritual bliss and economic prosperity. After his father's forty-year kingship,

Solomon inherited the throne and became the third generation to reign forty years over Israel. Solomon, representing the last generation of truth, brought the kingdom to its apex of peace and prosperity, but he allowed the influx of idolatry and offered his descendants a frustrated kingdom that quickly divided. Jeroboam and Rehoboam, representing the fourth generation of the Israelite monarchy, served as kings of a divided kingdom.

In three generations, Israel grew into a great and wealthy nation. While from the outside Israel displayed her grandeur and gold to visitors such as the Queen of Sheba, inwardly the great nation was splintering with distress. The many years of supporting an expensive monarchy etched deep stress marks in the society. Heavy expenditures of labor and finances to fulfill the king's decrees coupled with a tremendous spiritual decline undermined Israel's inner strengths until fragmentation resulted in the fourth generation of the monarchy.

As these scriptural examples indicate, the sectarian cycle can often be described in general terms by three successive generations, each of which tends to develop characteristics that can be identified. With this pattern in mind, let us consider some lessons about the sectarian cycle as revealed by history.

2

Lessons From History

Let us briefly survey some major reformational or revival movements in the history of Christendom to analyze the sectarian cycle more closely, considering the growth, expansion, plateau, and decline of each movement. Starting with the beginning of Protestantism in the sixteenth century, we will examine trends and characteristics of successive generations within selected movements.

The Lutherans

In the month of March 1517, six months before Martin Luther's ninety-five theses would be posted on the door of the church in Wittenberg, the Fifth Lateran Council abandoned its efforts to reform the church. The five years of sessions dealing with church reformation terminated in frustration.[3] Years of rationalization, deeper thought, and less influence of God's Spirit had eroded the Catholic church into a state of corruption. Martin Luther's personal leader, Gilles of Vitterbe, criticized the corruption of the clergy and its materialistic ambitions as he opened the meeting with cries for renewal. However, every meeting closed in frustration because no solutions were found to the overwhelming problems. A great Roman Catholic historian summarized the result: "The times were not ripe for a profound transformation of manners in the Italy of the Renaissance. The corruptions of the Curia were not corrected. Pope Leo X, sunk in the utterly profane luxuries of his court and worship of the arts, remained inert in the face of the church's needs."[4]

God was attempting to direct the Catholic church away from corruption and guide it into depths of truth. Because of inward selfishness, the ministerial leadership rejected God's gentle leading, and God turned to an obscure monk to lead him into greater truth. In six months, the ninety-five theses appeared on the door at Wittenberg, Germany. Soon, the torch of the Reformation was aflame, its blaze spreading throughout Western Christendom.

passivity. . . . [It was] a movement of revival, aimed at making man's relation to God experientially and morally meaningful as well as socially relevant."[9]

Offering life within a dead religious structure, a zeal for holiness and devotion to God in the place of dead faith, and warm divine experiences in the place of cold theological interpretations and worldliness, Pietism spread rapidly throughout Lutheranism.[10]

In 1546 Luther died; in 1566 the Lutheran movement reached its peak. By the middle of the seventeenth century, Lutheranism had lost most of its fervor and granted its inheritors a cold, dead body, creating the need for Pietism.

Establishing a trend that numerous other religious organizations would follow, the Lutheran church lost much of its initial fervor and influence in approximately one hundred years, following the basic pattern of the sectarian cycle. Many of its adherents plummeted from high standards of conduct and theology within about three generations. As one historian has concluded, in this period of time the Lutheran churches had almost completely lost their initial character and emphasis, yielding largely to pietistic expressions of the Christian faith.[11]

Puritanism

While in mainland Europe Lutheranism emerged out of a discontented Catholic church, a similar occurrence unfolded in England, creating the Church of England. The Puritan movement that arose out of the English Reformation experienced expansion, plateau, and decline within about three generations.

The intriguing stage for the English Reformation was set by King Henry VIII, who sought to divorce his wife. Doing so, however, would violate Catholic church ordinances, thereby provoking excommunication by Pope Clement VII and (by Catholic church standards) eternal damnation.

When the Reformation began in mainland Europe, King Henry VIII seized the opportunity to "reform" the Catholic church in England to satisfy his personal desires. By his royal power and influence, he severed all official ties with the Vatican. The Catholic church in England became the Church of England with King Henry VIII as the head instead of the pope.[12] Initially, then, the English Reformation was largely political rather than theological; the Church of England still retained most of the unscriptural beliefs and practices of the Roman Catholic Church while separating from it organizationally.

The English royal and parliamentary transactions that produced the Church of England,[13] rather than attacking the corruption of the church, offered a structure for enhanced immorality and impurity. However, by 1559, a large and vigorous reforming party was in existence, setting the stage for the triumph of Puritanism. For example, in 1578, Doctor Laurence Chaderton, one of the scholars responsible for the development of the King James Version of the Bible, dramatically condemned the king's church, stating that the church was "a huge mass of old and stinkinge workes, or conjuring, witchcraft, sorcery, charming, blaspheming the Holy name of God, swearing and forswearing, profaning of the Lord's Sabbothe, disobedience to superiours, contempt of inferiours; murther, manslaughter, robberies, adulterye, fornication, covenant-breaking, false witness-bearing, lieing," that it was filled with arrogant hypocrites and renegades, and that there was an urgent need everywhere for honest and zealous religious leaders "to admonish, correct, suspende, and excommunicate such noysome, hurtful, and monstrous beastes out of the house of God, without respect of persons."[14]

Deriving its name from its efforts to purify the Church of England, Puritanism began as an internal movement that attempted to cleanse the Church of England from beliefs and practices remaining from the Catholic church.[15]

The Puritan movement advanced with momentum. Its remarkable growth owed much to the early proponents' uncompromising desire to embrace biblical teachings. It overcame "decades of political and ecclesiastical upheaval," reversed centuries of spiritual decline, and solidified ecclesiastical and institutional traditions. Since the majority of the clergy and the laity of England's church remained "unreformed," Puritanism sought for true renewal, thus establishing its platform for growth.[16]

Despite its dynamic growth, the Puritan movement encountered opposition from within the Church of England. Taking the English throne in 1625, Charles I, whose wife was a Roman Catholic, reestablished many Roman Catholic influences and propagated persecution against the Puritans. Hence, a great Puritan migration to America occurred in the 1630s.[17]

Although America's first colony, Jamestown, founded in 1607, was established as an English commercial endeavor, it was affected by Puritan influences. The colony's foundational philosophy is carved on a monument at the site of the first settlement: "Lastly and chiefly, the way to prosper and achieve good success is to make yourselves all of one mind for the good of your country and your own, and to serve and fear God, the Giver of all goodness, for every plantation which our

Heavenly Father hath not planted shall be rooted out."[18]

The founding philosophy of Jamestown developed into more than an admonishment only when Puritan personnel arrived after the devastating winter of 1610. Disease and starvation characterized Jamestown's economic condition, and its spiritual despair was made evident in that the church house became a "dilapidated chapel." The spiritual and economic decline continued until a new governor, Thomas Dale, and a new clergyman, Alexander Whitaker, arrived in 1611 emphasizing Puritan principles.

Under Puritan influence, army officers were commanded to see "that the Almightie God be duly and daily served" and that those who missed morning and evening prayers be disciplined. Men elected to draft laws governing civil behavior conducted their business in the choir loft of Jamestown's church house. This assembly passed laws requiring discipline for idleness and gambling, fines for swearing, and public reprimand of the unruly if necessary. Every man and woman was required to attend morning and afternoon services on Sunday and participate in two daily devotions at the church house. Immoderate apparel was forbidden, slothfulness was punished, and persistent sinning resulted in excommunication and arrest. Zealous evangelism was promoted among the Indians, with Whitaker personally pursuing the conversion and baptism of Pocahontas. In a follow-up measure of this missionary endeavor, the people of Jamestown were admonished to educate a certain number of natives and prepare them for college.

With a conservative lifestyle legislated into civil code, spiritual and economic conditions of Jamestown began to blossom. "The fact remains that a period of Puritanical strenuousness was entered upon, and the colony for the first time began to show signs of stability. To the writer of *The New Life in Virginia* (1612), prospects were 'good.' "[19]

While Jamestown was adopting Puritan philosophies, a group of Puritans in England sought refuge from persecution. Ultimately, on November 21, 1620, a voyage across the Atlantic culminated with a landing off the coast of Cape Cod. Aboard the small sailing vessel, the eligible and able men had gathered in the cabin of the *Mayflower* and signed the Mayflower Compact to unite themselves "solemnly and mutually in the presence of God, and one of another" into one civil body. Incorporated in the Compact was their purpose: "Having undertaken for the glorie of God, and the advancement of the Christian faith, and honour of our King and countrie, a voyage to plant the first colonie in the Northern parts of Virginia. . . . "[20]

With a month's energies expended in searching for a location possessing sufficient natural resources and a potential for strong self-defense, the Pilgrim fathers agreed to settle in a desolate forest area, now known as Plymouth, Massachusetts, and there they unloaded the *Mayflower's* cargo through icy winter waters. This cold greeting served only as a sobering introduction to a devastating winter.

In the first winter, more than half of the men, thirteen of the eighteen women, and nineteen of the twenty-nine singles died. Only three married couples remained unbroken,[21] and only nineteen of the forty-one men who signed the Mayflower Compact survived.[22]

With great trust in God even while plagued with death, the Pilgrims refused to complain, and in the midst of the first winter's tragedies the Pilgrims acknowledged God's providence. They expressed gratitude for the freedom to worship God, the land in which they lived, and the friendliness they found in the Indians. Although many had died, the Pilgrims were thankful that many of the sick had recovered.

The Pilgrims' day began with prayer, and then breakfast was served. They esteemed Sunday as a day of Sabbath and dedicated it to prayer and meditation. The Pilgrim community collectively embraced the "Holy Discipline," a disciplined lifestyle that they felt would be pleasing to God. Serving God in America, the Pilgrims considered their existence an "opportunity of freedom and libertie to injoye ye ordinances of God in puritie."[23]

In 1626 Roger Conant persuaded a group of twenty fishermen whose business had collapsed to establish a colony in New England. This Dorchester Company founded Salem, Massachusetts, which became a city of refuge for migrating Puritans. On September 6, 1628, John Endecott directed about forty Puritans to Salem, beginning a great Puritan migration.

In England, a Dorchester clergyman named John White, possessing a tremendous missionary zeal coupled with his Puritan convictions, inspired several influential Puritans to form a new company. In March 1629 Charles I granted a charter to these persuasive Puritans, allowing the formation of the Massachusetts Bay Company. Four ships carrying three hundred Puritans and three qualified clergymen arrived in Massachusetts in June and July of 1629.[24] At the onset of this great migration and after two special "days of Humiliation," the people of Salem prepared and signed a document emphasizing their devotion to God. Writing what is known as the Salem Church Covenant, the Salem Puritans stated, "We Covenant with the Lord and one with an other; and doe bynd our selves in the presence of God to walke together in all his waies, according as he is pleased to reveale himself unto us in his blessed word of truth."[25]

Conservative in lifestyle, congregational in church governmental structure, and possessing strict moral standards and missionary zeal, the early Puritans arrived by the thousands in America. In 1630 John Winthrop spearheaded a massive migration of nearly a thousand Puritans from England to Massachusetts Bay. By 1641 at least another twenty thousand had followed. The great influx of people altered the profile of the colony to the extent that the population center shifted to the harbor at the mouth of the Charles River, and Boston became the seat of government.[26] The early socioeconomic and spiritual fabric of America owed much to the conservativeness of first- and second-generation Puritans.

A closer observation of these congregational believers reveals interesting characteristics of the first and second generation of Puritans and provides insight into aspects of early American society. The early Puritans insisted the church should consist only of "visible saints" and their children. To be a saint, a person first had to make a knowledgeable profession of faith; then consistent God-fearing appearance and behavior were necessary requirements to display visibility.[27] In other words, a standard of conduct and dress became a criterion for maintaining church membership. For example, any person arrayed in silks and flounces (strips of fabric attached by one edge to the clothing) was judged to be "antichristian."[28] Sunday's agenda consisted of morning and afternoon services that were comprised of disharmonious songs, long prayers, and a lengthy sermon. The preaching explained Bible doctrines and stressed the practical applications of theology in daily living.

As their theology solidified, the Puritans developed experiential requirements for adult membership. Implementing a conviction that had existed for many years in most private circles, by 1635 the Bay Company leaders decided that men and women had to offer credible evidence of their personal experience of God's regenerating grace and inward divine calling. "For the first time in Christendom, a state church with vigorous conceptions of enforced uniformity in belief and practice was requiring an internal, experiential test of church membership." With only church members permitted to possess stock in the Massachusetts Bay Franchise and serve in government,[29] conservative, congregational Puritanism was experiencing its peak in America.

While the Puritan movement succumbed to the sectarian cycle and eventually declined, its effect in establishing conservative ideology in colonial

America was profound. It has been estimated that at least seventy-five percent of those declaring independence in 1776 were affected by Puritan influences, and eighty-five to ninety percent would not be an extravagant estimate.[30]

The Puritan movement in America encountered at least five major problems that required reconsideration of theological and organizational standards. By the middle of the seventeenth century, the second-generation leaders were forced to deal with these difficulties, which produced some devastating results.

The first problem involved a theological question concerning the amount and degree of rigid rules that should be placed on believers. The many regulations provided an opportunity for hypocrisy and inconsistent behavior. The Puritan theological structure, based much on human rationalism, eventually fell under question, diluting the momentum of the movement. The intellectual reasoning capabilities of man erected an edifice that it would also ultimately destroy.

A second difficulty revolved about the philosophy and practice of separatism. The Puritan fathers embraced the marriage of church and state, a philosophy inherited from England; however, Rhode Island, founded by Roger Williams, and Pennsylvania, founded by William Penn, promoted separation of church and state.

A third problem facing the Puritan leaders was the interrelationships of Puritan churches. Although in theory the Puritan churches were uniform, practical problems regarding church government and disciplines led to a meeting of the clergy. In September 1646 the Cambridge Synod, as it became known, began sessions that sought greater uniformity of the churches. Agreement was obtained, and the church's structure crystallized.

The fourth adverse situation involved the native Indian population. Varying attitudes concerning Indian land rights and evangelism efforts among the Indians drove Puritans to opposing sides.

Directly influenced by the first four previously mentioned problems, the fifth predicament facing the Puritans was decreased fervency. With diminished zeal, the privilege of being a Puritan developed into a burden, and the lifestyle of being a Puritan was reduced to a routine. The process of routinization resulted in diminishing fervor and decline.[31]

Diminishing feelings of experience, emotion, and expression grew obvious. As one historian put it, "Among the second and later generations of Puritans (as well as among the immigrants who continued to arrive) there were many duly baptized members to whom the experience of saving grace never came."[32]

Without a nourishing influx of "visible saints," greater tendencies toward rationalism and intellectualism developed, and discord increased through the 1650s. "In 1657, a Connecticut-Massachusetts ministerial council met and approved certain 'half-way' measures." Dealing with questions of church membership, the Half-Way Covenant compromised some of the Puritans' strong stands.[33]

As the Puritan movement's deterioration continued, accompanied by growing anguish among the clergy, declining piety eroded the Puritan foundation. "As New England stood at the threshold of the eighteenth century, the religious situation as a whole exhibited a static quality. . . . Where the fires of religious enthusiasm once had burned so brightly, a . . . status quo had won acceptance and . . . the drift to quiescence was equally noticeable."[34] On the brink of the Great Awakening, "worldly Puritans" became numerous and outspoken.

The cyclic situation was summarized by an aphorism that Cotton Mather had quoted in his survey of the Plymouth Colony: *Religio peperit Divitics, Filia devoravit Matrem,* that is, "Religion brought forth prosperity, and the daughter destroyed the mother." He proceeded to state, "There is danger lest the enchantments of this world make them to forget their errand into the wilderness."[35]

The Great Awakening

In 1734 in Northampton, Massachusetts, Jonathan Edwards preached powerful messages of renewal, and a great revival mushroomed. The community experienced the beginnings of what came to be called the Great Awakening. In a letter to Benjamin Coleman of Boston, Edwards wrote, "This town never was so full of love, nor so full of joy, nor so full of distress as it has lately been. . . . I never saw the Christian spirit in love to enemies so exemplified, in all my life as I have seen it within this half-year." Edwards credited the work of the Holy Spirit and the preaching of sound doctrine as the cause of renewal.[36]

The revival that started in Northampton quickly spread throughout adjacent towns. Soon the whole Connecticut River Valley experienced a marvelous religious renewal. "From Northfield to Saybrook Point, the religion stirrings of Northampton were known."[37]

The flamboyant preaching of the circuit-riding evangelist George Whitefield propagated the Great Awakening to spiritually hungry America. In 1739 Whitefield's circuit gradually enlarged from Philadelphia to New York, through the middle colonies, and to Georgia in the South. As Whitefield began preaching in New England, his evaluation of New England's religious condition was pessimistic: "I am verily persuaded, the Generality of Preachers talk of an unknown, unfelt Christ. And the reason why Congregations have been so dead is because dead men preach to them." However, before Whitefield left New England in 1740, he preached to overflow crowds exceeding eight thousand people.[38]

During the years of 1740-1743, the powerful revivals of Whitefield, Tennent, and Davenport, accompanied by the efforts of lay itinerant preachers, propelled New England into "a great and general Awakening." In some of the more strict preaching of the Great Awakening, Davenport ordered that "wigs, cloaks, rings, and other vanities be burned."[39]

The dynamic and highly emotional preaching caused many conversions and often intense bodily demonstration. Fainting, weeping, shrieking, and shouting exuberantly shook dead churches. Experiential faith replaced the routine formalism that had gripped the congregations of New England. Once again, churches emphasized the need for adult members to have an inward experience of redemptive grace. "Preaching, praying, devotional reading, and individual 'exhorting' took on new life. In spite of far more demanding requirements, the increase in church membership is estimated variously between twenty and fifty thousand."[40]

John Wesley, the English founder of Methodism, also toured America, issuing cries for renewal and enhancing evangelical expansion in the southern colonies. Although he spent most of his time and energy in the British Isles, he made a powerful impact in America. Preaching that it is possible to fall from grace and opposing the doctrine of unconditional eternal security, he also declared that every sincere believer should possess an energetic drive to be holy, sanctified, and victorious over sin. "He produced regulations about clothes, food and drink, ornaments, money, buying and selling, and language. There was strict corporate and personal discipline; victories and defeats were reported, . . . and offenders excommunicated. . . . Wesley himself expelled sixty-four members for a variety of sins ranging from swearing and Sabbath breaking to vaguer categories such as 'idleness, railing, lightness, etc .' "

An incredible zeal burned the heart of the converted. In what is considered one of the greatest consequences of the Great Awakening, the clergy awakened to the potential of the laity's involvement in personal evangelism. The laity assumed many functions formerly restricted to pastors, and greater evangelization occurred. Evangelistic enthusiasm gripped the first generation of the Great Awakening.

Eventually, the revivals of the Great Awakening sadly followed the pattern observed in previous religious movements. In a short period of time, the Awakening reached its climax and began to decline in the second generation.

Jonathan Edwards Jr. serves as an example of this decline. Following in the footsteps of his father, he entered the ministry upon his graduation from Princeton University. Giving way to intellectualism and rationalization, the young Edwards introduced "one of the most intricate and pathetic exhibitions of theological reasoning which the history of Western thought affords."[42] Although the primary purpose was to defend his father and teachers, his theological reasoning led to tragic results:

> The profound tragedy of Edwards' theology was transformed into a farce by his would-be disciple [his son], who used his language and ignored his piety. . . . Edwards' "true virtue" was buried under a mass of distinctions invented in order to make the church acceptable to men of secondary virtue. . . . Holy love faded into conformity to the moral law, and such conformity was not the measure and substance of "true virtue." Such bleak and cruel Calvinism was doomed in New England, when . . . a humanized liberalism won the day, and introduced a

softer note into the religious life of New England. . . . Its holy fire was quenched, and its theological ashes lay exposed to the four winds, . . . the logic being transformed into a vast, complicated, and theological structure, bewildering to its friends, and ridiculous to its enemies.[43] The young Edwards "sought refuge in compromise, endeavoring to reconcile what was incompatible."[44]

In this way, the Great Awakening began its decline on the vehicle of intellectualism and rationalization. The powerful revival movement died a premature death before the third generation had an opportunity to develop fully in the way of their grandfathers.

The premature death occurred primarily because "after 1760, Americans were increasingly preoccupied by issues of government, law, trade, war, and nation-building—not theology."[45] Because of the Revolutionary War, the sectarian cycle was interrupted and accelerated in the midst of the second generation.

The Second Awakening

Again with America's spirituality and piety at a low, God focused His love and attention toward those who were hungry for truth. Between 1797 and 1801, the Second Awakening shook many towns of New England from Connecticut to New Hampshire. Edward Dorr Griffin described the movement from his perspective: "I saw a continued succession of heavenly sprinklings at New Salem, Farmington, Middleburg, and New Hartford . . . until, in 1799, I could stand at my door in New Hartford, Litchfield County, and number fifty to sixty contiguous congregations laid down in one field of divine wonders."[46]

The revival fires spread to Cane Ridge, Kentucky, on August 6, 1801, through the ministry of Barton Warren Stone. With crowds estimated from ten to twenty-five thousand people, many people regarded this revival as "the greatest outpouring of the Spirit since Pentecost."[47] Barton Stone himself stated: "Many things transpired there which were so much like miracles, that if they were not, they had the same effects as miracles on infidels and unbelievers; for many of them by these were convinced that Jesus was the Christ, and bowed in submission to him."[48] He also recorded some intriguing descriptions of spiritual, emotional, and physical experiences of the Second Awakening:

> The bodily agitations or exercises, attending the excitement in the beginning of this century, were various, and called by various

names. . . . The falling exercise was very common among all classes, the saints and sinners of every age and of every grade, from the philosopher to the clown. The subject of this exercise would, generally, with a piercing scream, fall like a log on the floor, earth, or mud, and appear as dead. . . .

The jerks cannot be so easily described. Sometimes the subject of the jerks would be affected in some one member of the body, and sometimes the whole system. When the head alone was affected, it would be jerked backward and forward, or from side to side, so quickly that the features of the face could not be distinguished. When the whole system was affected, I have seen the person stand in one place, and jerk backward and forward in quick succession, their head nearly touching the floor behind and before. All classes, saints and sinners, the strong as well as the weak, were thus affected. . . .

The dancing exercise. This generally began with the jerks, and was peculiar to the professors of religion. The subject, after jerking awhile, began to dance, and then the jerks would cease. Such dancing was indeed heavenly to the spectators; there was nothing in it like levity, nor calculated to excite levity in the beholders. The smile of heaven was shown on the countenance of the subject, and assimilated to angels appeared the whole person. Sometimes the motion was quick and sometimes slow. Thus they continued to move forward and backward in the same track or alley till nature seemed exhausted, and they would fall prostrate on the floor or earth, unless caught by those standing by. While thus exercised, I have heard their solemn praises and prayers ascending to God.

The barking exercise, (as opposers contemptuously called it,) was nothing but the jerks. A person affected with the jerks, especially in his head, would often make a grunt, or bark, if you please, from the suddenness of the jerk. . . .

The laughing exercise was frequent, confined solely with the religious. It was loud, hearty laughter, but one sui generis; it excited laughter in none else. The subject appeared rapturously solemn, and his laughter excited solemnity in saints and sinners. It is truly indescribable.

The running exercise was nothing more than, that persons feeling something of these bodily agitation, through fear, attempted to run away, and thus escape from them; but it commonly happened that they ran not far, before they fell, or became so greatly agitated that they could proceed no farther. . . .

I shall close this chapter with the singing exercise. This is more unaccountable than any thing else I ever saw. The subject in a very happy state of mind would sing most melodiously, not from the mouth or nose, but entirely in the breast, the souls issuing from thence. Such music silenced every thing, and attracted the attention of all. It was most heavenly. None could ever be tired of hearing it. . . .

The good effects were seen and acknowledged in every neighborhood.[49]

The results of the Second Awakening were staggering. Among the amazing accomplishments, the Sunday school program of evangelizing and discipling children was established and broadened.

The Second Awakening preaching stressed conversions that produced moral restoration and radical change of behavior. Obscenity, profanity, and drunkenness were categorized as despicable behavior. The movement grew, and by 1826 a national organization monitored restrictions on Sunday activities, dancing and theater going became increasingly questionable, and lotteries were banned.

Accompanying the Second Awakening was an age of humanitarian reform. Driven by a passion for Christian charity and philanthropy, reformers challenged the practice of slavery, and ultimately society granted many rights to women and blacks. Individual religious rights served as the launching pad of this age of humanitarian progress.

As in previous revivals, an exuberant missionary zeal gripped the hearts of believers. This energetic fervency to evangelize dazzled the world when in 1812 a group of foreign missionaries set sail for India. Several missionary societies were then established, producing a phenomenal expansion of the churches.[50]

The zeal for evangelization was also observed in America. For example, a glance at the Methodist church (which had its American roots when John Wesley introduced the message to Georgia) offers revealing statistics. At the beginning of the nineteenth century the Methodist church claimed 2,622 white and 179 black members in the whole western country. By 1812, there were 29,093 white and 1,648 black Methodists, while the circuits had increased from nine to sixty-nine. By 1830 the number of conferences west of the Alleghenies had increased to eight; the membership had grown from 30,000 to more than 175,000, among which were nearly 2,000 Indians and more than 15,000 blacks.[51]

Like other revival movements, the Second

Awakening reached a climax and then declined. The diminishing trend was first evident in the Methodist camp meeting, the great machine that produced much of the Methodist expansion. By the 1840s, the original excitement of the camp meeting was dying and more permanent buildings replaced the tents. In later years the camp meeting developed into a time of enjoyable vacationing at a resort.[52]

The decline of the Second Awakening continued throughout the dispute over slavery and the Civil War. While economic and political reconstruction occurred after the Civil War, moral corruption and scandal ransacked the countryside. In 1883 Henry George stated in *Social Problems:*

> The rapid changes now going on are bringing up problems that demand the most earnest attention . . . . Symptoms of danger, premonitions of violence, are appearing all over the civilized world. Creeds are dying, beliefs are changing; the old forces of conservatism are melting away. It is the new wine beginning to ferment in old bottles.[53]

The problem of decline was addressed in 1870 when the Methodist convention, in the face of the moral looseness, called its membership to repentance. Wesleyan sanctification and every aspect of its lifestyle were to be reestablished. By 1876, however, the Methodist church included an increasingly affluent membership. Consequently, the teachings against elaborate apparel, fine church buildings, organs, and choirs passed away. The church lost contact with the urban poor, and a stronger middle- and upper-class constituency developed. The Industrial Revolution coupled with Civil War issues and aftereffects drew the spotlight away from the prohibitions on dancing, tobacco, alcoholic beverages, gambling, card playing, and theater going.[54]

Following the sectarian cycle, the Second Awakening was born, blossomed by great growth until it reached a peak, and then began to decline. The foundation was laid for a new movement— the Holiness movement.

The Holiness Movement

Amid an increasingly corrupt nation, while U. S. Grant served as the president of the United States, the Holiness movement emerged; in 1867 the National Camp Meeting Association for the Promotion of Holiness was established. This revival began primarily among Wesleyans in an effort to retain or revive the conservative theology and lifestyle characteristic of original Methodism.

49

Vibrant growth marked the first generation of this movement, both by encompassing many established churches and by evangelizing the unchurched. Because of the accelerated growth rate and the diversity of peoples, no single denomination could bridle the Holiness movement, and in the second-generation efforts to organize, many splinter groups evolved. The first and second generations of the movement were characterized by a strict code of personal morality, abstinence from worldly pleasures and amusements, and requirements for believers to dress in modest apparel.

Like other movements before it, the Holiness movement fell captive to cyclic trends. In less than one hundred years, after World War II, the numerical growth and material prosperity of the majority led to compromise. With the relaxing of personal disciplines, the progeny of the Holiness movement began to dress fashionably regardless of modesty considerations, adorn themselves extravagantly, and participate in worldly entertainments.[55] Thus, the sectarian cycle was complete.

The Pentecostal Movement

Beginning in the early morning hours of January 1, 1901, the Holy Spirit fell upon Bethel Bible College in Topeka, Kansas, whose founder and leader was Charles F. Parham, a Holiness preacher. After many days of prayer, fasting, and study, Agnes N. Ozman, a student, became the first one there to receive the gift of the Holy Spirit with the initial evidence of speaking in a new language.[56] The revival soon spread to parts of Kansas, Missouri, and Texas.

In 1906 the revival spread through Houston, Texas, to Los Angeles, California, and a great outpouring of the Spirit fell on the Azusa Street Mission, pastored by William J. Seymour. The Azusa Street Mission radiated the Pentecostal message to all areas of the country, first to Missouri, North Carolina, Tennessee, Alabama, Georgia, and Florida, and then in every direction.

Accompanying the revival fires of this first generation of Pentecostals were the basic beliefs in speaking with tongues, divine healing, strict codes of personal behavior, conservative theology, the infallibility of Scripture, premillennialism, and the universal atoning grace of Christ.[57] Similar in many ways to the converts of the Great Awakening and Second Awakening, the Pentecostals were transformed both inwardly and outwardly by their spiritual experience.

The growth phase of the Pentecostal movement, marked by tremendous fervency, had its footing where the Holiness movement had developed. The movement then accelerated in growth and multiplied, covering much of North America and then spreading rapidly to foreign lands.

As the movement blossomed in numbers, a growing need for some kind of organization became evident. In December 1913 Eudorus N. Bell, publisher of *Word and Witness* in Malvern, Arkansas, and Howard A. Goss, pastor in Hot Springs, Arkansas, summoned all "saints who believe in the baptism with the Holy Ghost" to meet in April 1914 in Hot Springs to develop a more effective organizational means to coordinate and promulgate Pentecostalism.

The Pentecostals who gathered for the conference first gave themselves to three days of devotional services. Then, with phenomenal unity, the three hundred participants elected a governing body of presbyters and adopted the name of Assemblies of God. The strength of this new Pentecostal body is evident from the number of subscriptions to the new official periodical: twenty-five thousand. Bell became part of the faculty of a newly founded school as well as the chairman of the General Council.[58]

Other Pentecostal organizations also formed, and some previously established Holiness denominations became Pentecostal. Growth continued, but the sectarian cycle was also in evidence. In celebrating the seventy-fifth anniversary of the Assemblies of God, C. M. Ward, a respected leader within the Assemblies of God, expressed his concern about changes in direction:

> We started out as extreme congregationalists, and now we are moving toward episcopacy. If the tide isn't turned, we'll become one of the most rootless families in the church because liberty and freedom, our great heritage, will be lost. . . . The result [in Assemblies of God colleges] is that today, with only a few exceptions, very few students want to become preachers. They want to be staff members, educators—something comfortable that assures employment.[59]

A respected historian has summarized the organizational advancement as well as some significant changes in trinitarian Pentecostalism:

> They were holding well-organized world conferences, and actively participated in the National Association of Evangelicals and were represented by two small Chilean churches in the World Council of Churches. They had become interested in advanced theological education, and had begun to experience internal dissension because of these accommodationist tendencies. As if to dramatize this trend, Oral Roberts, who rose to na-

tional fame as a Pentecostal preacher, healer, and television sensation, had become a Methodist in 1965.[60]

In the late 1960s and early 1970s, in a nation marred by the seemingly endless Vietnam War, racial riots, rebellion, and the emergence of a youthful counterculture, a fresh wave of religious fervor swept through the country. Labeled the charismatic movement, it had begun in the late 1950s and it involved individuals from various mainline denominations, Full Gospel groups, and antiestablishment Jesus People who received the Holy Spirit with the sign speaking in tongues.[61] Initially, the charismatics remained within their traditional denominations and emphasized brotherly love and unity over doctrine. From the practice of speaking with tongues and the belief that Christians may demonstrate spiritual gifts (Greek, *charismata*), the movement received its name.

Over the years, much of the trinitarian Pentecostal movement has aligned itself closely with the charismatic movement. Modern trinitarian Pentecostals have altered or abandoned many of the disciplines and standards of the early Pentecostal believers, and in many cases have begun to place less emphasis on doctrines once embraced as dear. Once again, the sectarian cycle is in evidence.

3

The Oneness Pentecostal Movement

The Pentecostal movement cannot be analyzed solely by looking at the trinitarian Pentecostals, for beginning in 1913 and 1914 many people in the first generation of Pentecostalism rediscovered the important scriptural truths of the oneness of God, the absolute deity of Jesus Christ, and water baptism in the name of Jesus.

Although opposed by trinitarian Pentecostals, including the Assemblies of God, this new movement rejected human religious traditions and relied upon Scripture to proclaim the doctrine known today as Oneness. Denying the existence of three divine persons of a trinity, Oneness Pentecostals hold that God is absolutely one and that Jesus is the fullness of the Godhead incarnate (Deuteronomy 6:4; Colossians 2:9). Thus, Jesus is the Father incarnate, and the Holy Spirit is the Spirit of Jesus. Instead of baptizing converts in the titles of Father, Son, and Holy Spirit, Oneness Pentecostals emphatically teach that everyone should be baptized "in the name of Jesus Christ" (Acts 2:38).

The Oneness doctrine maintains that there is one God, who has revealed Himself to humanity in various ways: A singular God created everything, robed Himself in flesh to pay the price necessary to redeem fallen humanity, and abides in Spirit form in the hearts of believers. It also embraces the name of Jesus as the identification of this single God as manifested in the flesh for our salvation. This truth is expressed in the words of a simple song that many Oneness believers sang:

I'm so glad I've found it out, I found it out in time:
I know Jesus is the Father,
I know Jesus is the Son,
I know Jesus is the Holy Ghost,
And all these three are one!

To the early Oneness Pentecostals, accepting the Oneness message was predicated upon a glorious touch of God on their lives and a scriptural understanding of the sovereignty and identity of God.

Although some Pentecostal leaders such as Charles Parham had baptized converts in Jesus' name earlier, 1913-1914 marks the beginning of Oneness Pentecostalism as a distinct movement. In 1913 R. E. McAlister noted publicly that the apostles baptized in Jesus' name, and in 1914 Frank Ewart and Glenn Cook began rebaptizing people in Jesus' name. The Jesus Name formula and the associated teaching of Oneness spread rapidly throughout Pentecostalism.

Some Pentecostal preachers embraced the Jesus Name message with little or no initial contact from others. For example, in 1914, Evangelist C. A. Pyatt, a young preacher in his early twenties, was preaching a nine-month revival in Mena, Arkansas, and hundreds received the Holy Ghost. After preaching on a Friday night, Evangelist Pyatt prayed all night, and in the early hours of Saturday morning, through prayer and Bible study, he received the Jesus Name message. In the Saturday night revival service, he preached the message to the people and asked for those who desired to be baptized in the name of Jesus to meet him at the water's edge Sunday evening to be rebaptized.

About seventy people gathered to be baptized in Jesus' name that next day.[62]

Similarly, A. D. Urshan, a Persian immigrant to America, received an understanding of baptism in Jesus' name while evangelizing throughout Russia in 1915. He had been converted to Pentecostalism while in America and later returned to Persia to share his testimony with his family and friends. Because of a lost passport, his return to America led him to the Russian Embassy and then on a route through Russia. He preached in several cities in Russia and saw many people receive the Holy Spirit. Some of his converts requested him to baptize them in Jesus' name according to the Book of Acts, and he himself was rebaptized in Jesus' name while in Russia. From that time until his death, he preached that Jesus was God and baptized converts in the name of Jesus.[63]

So rapid and comprehensive was the spread of this so-called "New Issue," that the Assemblies of God debated the doctrine at a general convention in St. Louis, Missouri, in 1916. The organization adopted a strong trinitarian statement, which caused 156 ministers to leave the fellowship,[64] out of a total of 585. Among those who departed were two executive presbyters: Howard Goss and D. C. O. Opperman. E. N. Bell had briefly embraced the Jesus Name message and had even been rebaptized, but ultimately he decided to remain with the Assemblies of God and was later elected as general chairman again.

The Oneness Pentecostal movement maintained vibrant growth, even while experiencing immense persecution for denying the trinitarian doctrine. Growth flourished under the ministry of the first-generation preachers, whose commitment to the cause was unfettered by abuse or ridicule. Devoting themselves completely to the truth they loved and embraced, they formed a core that would propagate their understanding of Bible truths to their world.

As the movement grew, the second generation added organization to zeal, and various groups emerged. Resulting from a merger of the Pentecostal Assemblies of Jesus Christ and the Pentecostal Church, Incorporated, the United Pentecostal Church International became the largest Oneness group in the world.[65] Organizational structure provided unity in effort and spurred the movement into growth.

Presently, the Oneness Pentecostal movement is facing its third generation. Only time will declare if the movement will effectively succumb to the sectarian cycle, or defy the trend of history.

4

Characteristics of the
First Generation

As we analyze the sectarian cycle, let us seek
to identify some basic characteristics of the successive generations of a movement. Although not
every movement or individual will fit precisely
into these categories, some general trends are
apparent.

The first generation of a movement includes the
individuals who receive a new understanding of
truth or a spiritual experience. Several attributes
typically characterize the adherents who initially
build the foundation that grows into a Bible-based
religious movement: a genuine dedication to God,
a priority on the things of God, a God-centered pie-

ty, a dynamic missionary spirit, and a continual desire for personal spiritual growth.

First-generation believers give little consideration to personal desires, but their whole life revolves around God and His cause. An unrestricted dedication to God results in a lifestyle in which working for the cause of God is more important than anything else, and they seek to obey God's will regardless of the consequences.

As a part of their dedication to God, the first-generation pioneers of a movement place God first in everything—ambitions, finances, desires, and goals. Because of their priority on the things of God, they have no time or finances for "worldly" involvement. They expend all resources to build the kingdom of God; God is first in every detail of life. The founding fathers esteem God's cause, calling, and purpose as top priority, even over securing the basic needs of life. The first-generation pioneers do not care for earthly praise, stature, finance, fame, or power. They are only content if Jesus receives the glory He deserves.

Numerous examples in the history of the Oneness movement depict this lifestyle of complete dedication in which God's will is the priority. For instance, C. P. Kilgore sacrificed greatly to perpetuate the gospel in the south-central states. Traveling from town to town with his family of nine children, he preached the Oneness

The central thought embraced by the early Reformers was justification by faith. They recognized that people did not become just and righteous in the sight of God by performing an array of good deeds or by paying a given price for sin (penance); rather, justification came only by the work of Calvary and faith in Jesus Christ. The doctrine of justification by faith did not mean condoning a life of sin. To the contrary, Luther acknowledged that followers of Christ should seek to live a godly life.[5]

Lutheranism fermented and grew, sweeping from Germany throughout all Europe. By 1566, while the second generation of leaders served the movement, Lutheranism probably secured its greatest territorial acquisitions.[6]

With the growth and advancements of Lutheranism, eventually an intellectual tendency to control religion with reasoning abilities developed. Ultimately, "this religion of the warmed heart was soon followed or paralleled by an expression of the cool-headed intellect in the equally widespread movement called rationalism."[7] Rationalism engendered several devastating consequences within the Lutheran movement.

First, moral standards were compromised. Although the concept of justification by faith initially led people to pursue a life of holiness, many of the movement's descendants misused the same fundamental concept to erode moral ideals. Rationalizing that they could live as they wished and participate in any activities they desired, many people felt that by confessing belief in Jesus Christ they could still consider themselves righteous. Rationalization eroded the concept of justification by faith from purity and righteousness to license for sinfulness.

A second result of the rationalization trend was a crystallization process. Second-generation followers became discontented with the lack of organization and began establishing governmental structure, as well as structuring their theology.[8] Solidity in thinking and organization offered the platform for enhanced growth; however, after a season of increase, structure mushroomed into a burdensome edifice that inhibited growth and crystallized the movement.

Third, rationalism served to prepare for a new movement: Pietism. With increasingly lethargic and worldly character encouraged by rationalism in the second generation and predominating in the third generation, the stage was set for another religious wave. Combatting the corruption that had evolved from rationalization, Pietism reached against the apathetic attitude of the Lutheran church. Attempting to strengthen Christian piety and purity of life, Pietism protested against "intellectualism, church formalism, and an ethical

Pentecostal message: the lordship of Jesus, repentance, baptism in Jesus' name for the remission of sin, and the baptism of the Holy Spirit with the sign of speaking in tongues, and holiness of life. Many existing United Pentecostal churches in Oklahoma and Texas owe their existence to this man's efforts.[66]

The dedicated lifestyle of a pioneer preacher who established the first Oneness Pentecostal church in Oklahoma City, Oklahoma, exemplifies the daily life of this first generation. After working throughout the night in the oil fields of Oklahoma, he administrated and taught in the church school. Upon retiring from the daily activities of the Christian school, he would rest for only a few hours, usually returning to the church for revival service. After directing the service preliminaries and introducing the evangelist, he would lie down in the choir loft. Sleeping through the preaching, he would awaken to pray for needy individuals throughout the congregation. Praying and encouraging until everyone was finished, he returned to the oil field to work all night.

Day after day, year after year, he and his family survived on little finances and no modern conveniences. All his life's energies propelled God's purpose in Oklahoma City, and he allowed little time, money, or pleasure for self. The money he acquired from labor in the oil fields sustained the church/school operation, and he invested his life into the lives of others. In this environment of complete commitment, many converts also yielded their lives to ministerial service and contributed greatly to the growth of the United Pentecostal Church.[67]

Many other examples illustrate the same life drama—dedication to God and priority on the things of God. One after another, we can relate stories of consecrated forefathers who gave of themselves, prayed for hours, fasted weeks, lived on bare minimums for the kingdom's sake, and died with few earthly possessions but received manifold honors in accordance with heaven's unlimited treasure-house. Religious movements are built with such dedication as the primary component.

Our first-generation founding fathers possessed a God-centered piety. As converts they understood that they were born in sin and that their righteousness was only as filthy rags (Isaiah 64:6). They knew that all the good deeds they could ever accomplish could never have lifted them out of their sinful condition or made them righteous in God's sight.

The first generation had a powerful encounter with the saving grace of God. They knew that God loved humanity so much that He robed himself in flesh and came to our level as Jesus Christ, the

Son of God. Conceived by the Holy Ghost, Jesus was sinless. He was made "in the likeness of sinful flesh, and for sin" (Romans 8:3), but He was holy, without spot or blemish. He was perfect.

This holy, spotless Lamb of God died a cursed death on Calvary and by so doing accepted the curse of humanity's fall, the curse of death. He took upon himself God's wrath for sin as he became the propitiation for sins.

Those who identify with the death, burial, and resurrection of Jesus Christ appropriate to their lives the blood of this spotless Lamb and so inherit everlasting life. Since Jesus bore transgressions, iniquities, and sin on the cross, the born-again believer is made "holy and unblameable and unreproveable" in the sight of God (Colossians 1:22).

Humanity was hopeless, but Jesus Christ, who is God incarnate, died and offered hope. When a person receives the benefits of the death of Jesus Christ, he is counted as righteous in God's sight. At the new birth the filthy, unrighteous person who could do nothing for himself becomes holy and righteous by the act of God.

The first generation of Oneness Pentecostals understood that God had made them holy, and their piety was a lifestyle of maintaining what God had established as holy. Since God had paid the price to make them holy, the believers' great responsibility was to walk in the holiness that God had imparted. They embraced numerous scriptural passages that taught holiness: "Come out from among them, and be ye separate" (II Corinthians 6:17). "Know ye not that ye are the temple of God, and that the Spirit of God dwelleth in you? If any man defile the temple of God, him shall God destroy; for the temple of God is holy, which temple ye are" (I Corinthians 3:16-17). "Be not conformed to this world: but be ye transformed by the renewing of your mind" (Romans 12:2). "Be ye holy; for I am holy" (I Peter 1:16).

The pioneers of the movement refrained from sin to prevent defiling what God had cleansed. To them, living a holy life consisted not of refraining from activities to make them holy, but refraining from ungodly activities to remain undefiled and to express God's holiness, of which they were partakers (Hebrews 12:10). Just as Almighty God could never touch anything unholy because it would defile Him, so the redeemed person did not desire to touch anything unclean because he too would be defiled.

The first-generation believers did not merely follow standards of holiness, but they patterned their lives after Matthew 6:33: "Seek ye first the kingdom of God, and his righteousness." Prayer, fasting, personal devotion, and Bible reading were all part of seeking His righteousness. Maintaining a holy life consisted also of following Philippians 4:8: "Finally, brethren, whatsoever things are true, whatsoever things are honest, whatsoever things are just, whatsoever things are pure, whatsoever things are lovely, whatsoever things are of good report; if there be any virtue, and if there be any praise, think on these things."

More important than the activities they refrained from were the daily activities in which the first generation involved themselves. As a result, righteousness and piety were God-centered in the mind of the first generation.

Fourth, first-generation converts typically have a dynamic missionary zeal. The missionary zeal of the Puritans and Pilgrims reached toward the Indians. The Great Awakening reached all of North America. The Second Awakening sent missionary parties to India, and the Pentecostal revival dispatched missionaries to the whole world.

Not only do they have a foreign missionary zeal, but the first-generation converts share with anybody and everybody the good news of the gospel. With great excitement, enthusiasm, and thanksgiving for what Jesus has done in his personal life, the new convert desires to tell everyone —his neighbors, friends, family, distant relatives, casual acquaintances—about Jesus Christ. Accompanying this verbal communication about Jesus Christ are prayer, fasting, and spiritual concern for the lost person.

The convert has genuine concern and love for lost souls, and reaching them with salvation truth is his paramount concern. Every society, neighborhood, and person soon knows of the life-transforming power of Jesus Christ, and numerical growth results.

The fifth attribute possessed by the first generation of believers is a continual desire for personal spiritual growth. Seemingly, they can never attain the depth in God they desire. Never satisfied with the current status of their personal relationship with God, they experience a yearning to grow deeper in God, climb higher with Jesus, and draw closer to Him. These desires lead to a greater dedication to God with more prayer, studying of the Bible, fasting, and personal and group devotions.

With a genuine dedication to God, a priority on the things of God, God-centered piety, a dynamic missionary zeal coupled with love, and a continual desire for personal spiritual growth, the first generation is composed of a solid core of believers who desire only the things of God and who live for the kingdom of God. Along with the numerical growth of the movement is a personal growth in the spiritual maturity of the believers. The solid foundation leads to the building of the second generation.

5

Characteristics of the Second Generation

The second generation of a Bible-based movement includes individuals who are children of those who first received a new understanding of truth or a spiritual experience. Typically, they are characterized by a genuine dedication to their parents. Often, however, this dedication to parents takes the place of supreme dedication to God Himself. In such a case, the religious experience of these second-generation people is characterized by a priority on the things of their parents, a parent-centered piety, mediocrity, crystallization, and the beginnings of rationalization. Let us examine these features in greater detail.

Giving little consideration to personal desires, the second generation of believers typically live the lifestyle in which they were raised. Their parents' dedication provoked conversion at an early age, and the children learned the routines of a dedicated lifestyle through parental example, instruction, and enforcement. By outside appearance, the first generation and second generation possess identical characteristics, but upon closer examination, distinct variations are often apparent.

The second-generation believers' dedication resembles the consecration of their parents. Their lifestyle appears identical to the first-generation converts. They wholeheartedly embrace the doctrines and beliefs in which they were raised.

Remaining in the second generation is a strong dedication to God, but it often exists as an indirect dedication to God. By comparison, the first generation was dedicated directly to God, but the second generation may be directly dedicated to their parents and indirectly dedicated to God. They are consecrated to God because their parents trained them to be, and they dare not deviate from their parents' teachings. Devotion and commitment soar because mothers and fathers emphasized their importance.

Just as with the first-generation believers, for the second generation church, little time or finances are available for "worldly involvement"; they expend all resources for the kingdom of God. Prayer, fasting, Bible reading, and personal devotion produce positive results within the second generation also, but instead of conducting these activities out of a personal love for God, many people in the second generation incorporate them from parental disciplines and maintain them by a love for the training and lifestyle they inherited.

Consecration based on parental guidance produces many positive results, as evidenced by the maintenance of the lifestyle of the first generation. Because the parents ingrained what to do and how to live into the children, the children, raised with a rigidly disciplined conscience, continually live their parents' life.

But indirect dedication to God will cause a second-generation person's lifestyle to result from parental guidance rather than personal, godly convictions. Without totally understanding why, he will maintain the life because Mother and Dad taught him to do so. Frequently, then, the second generation will adopt personal convictions that the first generation embraced, but without fully understanding the depth of experience in which those convictions developed.

Accompanying the dedication of the second generation to the parents' God is a priority on the things of the parents' God. Again, God still comes

71

first in everything, but often indirectly. To many in the second generation, the parents' ideals, ambitions, dreams, and commitments come first, and as a result they indirectly place priority on the things of God. After observing the price required of their parents to establish the work of God, they hold at top priority the maintenance of that effort.

The pioneers' children desire for the work established and paid for by the sweat and prayer of their parents to continue; however, if they lack genuine dedication to God, they will refuse to pay the extreme price that their parents did. An indirect priority on the things of God will be present: they want Christ to receive praise and glory. Also present will be a priority on parents: Mother and Dad deserve to receive some honor for their hard work. But often, the second generation, exhausted from giving everything and gaining nothing materially, desires some personal benefit. With a watered-down commitment, they place greater emphasis on structure. People begin to trust more in structure, thereby diluting a deep trust in God.

When this process occurs, the second generation possesses a parent-centered piety. Whereas, the first generation centered its righteousness and convictions on God, the second generation centers its righteousness and convictions on Mother and Dad.

Instead of refusing to partake in worldly activities because they are a violation of scriptural principles, the second generation often refuses to partake in worldly activities simply because their parents taught them they were wrong. Instead of rejecting the influence of worldly friends on the basis that such associations implant evil thoughts in their minds, the second generation often rejects them on the basis of what Mother and Dad taught them.

This process occurred to a great extent in the Holiness movement. Instead of refraining from immodest dress because it violated the Scripture, the second generation refrained from immodest dress because of parental teachings. Instead of women wearing their hair long to signify submission to God's plan as I Corinthians 11 teaches, daughters grew up with long hair because Mother and Dad taught that it was wrong to cut it. Instead of abstaining from alcohol and tobacco because they defiled God's holy temple and violated the Scripture, people abstained from alcohol and tobacco because of strict childhood training. Instead of refusing to read ungodly literature because it was not conducive to Christian thought or compatible with a holy lifestyle, the second generation refused to read such literature because their parents defined it as sin. Instead of possessing God-centered righteousness, the second generation possessed parent-centered piety.

The second generation often succumbs to the influence of mediocrity. For the sake of their parents, they retain a desire for the lost to be saved and they press on for the cause for which the first generation died. This pseudo-missionary spirit remains for several years until, after the decease of parents, the lack of genuine dedication causes personal zeal to give way to the rationalistic excuse that "somebody else can do it." This apathetic, lethargic spirit will continue to grow into the third generation.

The diminishing missionary fervor often follows amazing patterns. The missionary spirit exists for auxiliary reasons other than the need to reach lost humanity. In the second (and third) generation, the need still exists to reach lost people, but priorities of property, programs, and products serve often as the driving force instead.

To parent-centered believers, reaching people translates into more dollars. The more contributors, the more income for the church; and the focus of evangelism often shifts to obtaining property, such as nicer and bigger church plants. Pastors and church members often involve themselves primarily in building projects and displace the missionary zeal to reach the lost. For many within the second (and third) generation era of a movement, the evangelistic fervor has been so diluted that property improvements supposedly fulfill the great commission.

Second-generation adherents often focus on programs, weakening the priority of evangelizing people. Thus, these believers engage in an outreach program, fulfill all the necessary guidelines that are supposed to make the program effective, and forget the individuals that the program is attempting to reach. Individual needs of lost people actually become meaningless as the mechanics of the program provide guiltless pseudo-fulfillment of the command to evangelize. Operating a program takes priority over the lost, hurting people for whom the program was designed.

Believers of the second (and third) generation often feature their product over and above the needs of people. As an example, one day a needy man sat weeping and crying in a Oneness Pentecostal pastor's office seeking help and deliverance. When asked by the sinner how to find peace and freedom, the pastor offered a glorious explanation of God's plans and provisions. In a daze resulting from the whirlwind of theology, the sinner stood and walked out, never to be seen again by the pastor. Repeatedly the pastor sought forgiveness from God for placing his "product" of doctrine and Bible understanding in priority over a needy person. Supposedly he fulfilled the commission to evangelize by offering his holy product; however, the sinner was never converted. Very likely, the results would have been completely different if the pastor had targeted the sinner directly, empathizing with his pain and remorse and leading him directly to repentance. Instead, the pastor focused on his product as a result of diminished fervor and zeal to reach lost individuals.

Whereas the first generation continually sought a closer walk with God, the second generation often becomes satisfied with the status quo, thinking, We're saved, and that's what counts anyway. Complacency, mediocrity, and lethargy make inroads in the second generation, eroding the core of godly consecration and dedication.

The second generation is usually characterized by a crystallization process. Because of a great influx of believers and the problems of disorganization, the second generation establishes an organization and means of government. As necessary and helpful as it is, this organizational structure can provide the platform for rationalization that results in fundamental changes. No effective organizational structure can be established without a degree of higher thinking, and although it is beneficial and necessary, yet it sets the stage for potentially destructive rationalization.

In the second generation, the movement often reaches its peak in numbers and influence and then begins a descent. Decline begins on the vehicles of mediocrity and rationalization, which the third generation will champion until the movement completes the sectarian cycle and dies.

6

Characteristics of the Third Generation

The third generation of a movement consists to a great extent of grandchildren of those who first received a new understanding of truth or a spiritual experience and children of the generation that was primarily dedicated to parents. The movement of the third generation is often characterized by dedication to self, priorities placed on self, little or no missionary zeal, maintenance esteemed over evangelism, decreased desire for personal spiritual growth, rationalization or self-justification of compromising positions, self-centered piety, and crystallization.

Whereas the first-generation converts were completely dedicated to God and the second-generation believers were dedicated to their parents' beliefs, practices and teachings, third-generation followers are often dedicated to self. Although the complete structure stands as the skeleton of supernatural experience, and although God remains very much alive and worshiped, such people place self on the throne of the heart. The movement's pioneers gave little or no consideration to personal desires, and the second generation made some provision for the flesh, but third-generation adherents often give primary consideration to themselves. Actually, these people maintain greater dedication to themselves than they do to God.

Some dedication to God remains, but not at the expense of the dedication to self. People of the third generation typically attend church, support it financially, participate in Sunday school teaching or in the choir, assist the pastor in every way possible, and work in harmony with the church in its beliefs, standards, government, principles, and methodology—but only if church activities do not interfere with personal plans and objectives.

Church becomes an activity for social relationship. Instead of reaching sinners, many people spend efforts on impressing social friends. They place great importance upon fellowship and maintenance activities to preserve the social order. Instead of the desire to enhance their personal relationship with God, they exhibit a desire to enhance personal relationships with others.

Because of the dedication to self, church becomes primarily an activity of enjoyment, with emphasis on how well the choir sings or the preacher preaches. Youth programs, adult activities, and enjoyable, pleasurable events become tests of the effectiveness of the social program and quality of the church. People tend to dismiss anything burdensome (or hire someone else to do it), and enjoyment of churchgoing becomes the dominant concern.

Obviously, a priority on the things of self accompanies this dedication to self. Self-oriented people relegate God to a secondary place, next to self, and personal desires come first. For example, they will attend church if the family will not be enjoying a weekend of some other "family" activity. They will contribute finances to church-related efforts if doing so will not interfere with personal ambitions, such as recreational vehicles or activities and prestigious possessions that symbolize affluence, personal power, or prominence. Instead of developing a disciplined time of devotion in prayer and Bible reading, they reserve such expressions for spare time when it is convenient. Instead of devoting extra time to God, they devote more and more time to personal activities that bring personal relaxation, pleasure, and enjoyment.

For these people, the things of God still remain relatively high in priority: they attend church, love God, and maintain many beliefs. They raise their children in the church and continue their financial support, but they also accept many practices and ideas that their forefathers forcibly rejected. Although they think of God as extremely important, self seems to climb to a higher priority, and they compromise convictions, beliefs, and stands of their grandfathers.

Under these conditions, maintenance of the organization increases to a higher priority than evangelizing others. Careful scrutiny to keep the organization from deteriorating shifts the movement from an offensive, dynamic, growing body to a defensive, protective body, focused inwardly rather than outwardly.

With a diminished dedication to God, missionary zeal and desire for personal growth decreases. A satisfaction with a mediocre Christian lifestyle develops. Regardless of their personal experience with God or lack of it, many people believe that they obtain salvation and keep their spiritual status by living a good life, being a good person, and doing good things. They develop an apathetic attitude of allowing somebody else to win souls, reach the lost, carry the load, pray, and fast. It becomes satisfactory to attend church and selfishly absorb every benefit without shouldering any burden.

To pacify the guilt resulting from ignoring the great commission, these believers engage in activities that supposedly fulfill their obligation. By supporting missions financially, they feel that they have discharged their obligation to fulfill the great commission. By rallying around programs and property projects, they feel that they have completed their responsibility. Like many in the second generation, they target their product rather than people. They maintain certain biblical definitions more than evangelizing others.

Resulting from this lethargic mediocrity that silently slips into the movement, the church begins to crystallize as a social organization. Following trends that began in the second generation, the third generation believers often focus more on local "atmosphere" than "outmosphere." Instead of individuals attending church to mature in Christ, draw closer to God, and reach the lost, they attend to enjoy their friends, listen to the choir, enjoy the preaching, and trust everything is right with God. As meeting selfish needs becomes increasingly important, the principles upon which the movement was founded decrease in importance.

In general, the first generation possesses a strict standard of holiness based on a God-centered piety. By contrast, many in the third generation compromise certain standards and develop a code of conduct characterized by self-justification. This self-centered standard busily provides excuses for diminished aspects of commitment by focusing instead on positive behavior. Peer pressure, both from inside and outside the movement, becomes an important consideration.

As people concentrate on self, the concept often develops that believers can make themselves holy by proper philosophies or conduct, whereas the pioneers understood that they were made holy by God and that philosophies and conduct were outworkings of God's holiness. Most of the convictions of the first generation's piety remain, but these aspects often become forms of pharisaical self-righteousness. Many pioneer beliefs remain, but they often serve the purpose of making the third generation supposedly righteous in the eyes of God. This attitude leads to personal justification of wrong behavior and rationalization of sins of the spirit.

The first generation of believers understood that their righteousness came only by God through the blood of Christ, and they refused to participate in any activity that was a detriment to spirituality or a defilement of the holiness God had imparted. Many people in the third generation, however, may feel that they obtain and maintain righteousness by doing the right things and performing the right deeds. They justify a failure to be right inwardly by a list of theological propositions, and they convert true righteousness into mere behavioral codes.

The codes of conduct, drawn from convictions of grandparents, may appear identical to the lifestyle of the grandparents, but the grandchildren may follow them in an attempt to acquire salvation and holiness by works. The positive result of maintaining movement ideals exists simultaneously with the negative result of developing a self-centered religion.

Instead of refusing to partake in worldly activities because they violate scriptural passages and would defile what God had made "holy, unblameable, and unreprovable," the third generation may refuse to involve themselves in such activities only because they think proper conduct will give them righteousness in God's eyes. Instead of rejecting the influence of worldly friends on the basis that such association would implant evil thoughts into their minds, the third generation may reject negative friends on the basis that they are more righteous than the sinners. Instead of refusing to read ungodly books because they waste valuable time, lead away from God's righteousness, and lead to impure, dishonest, and evil thoughts, the third generation may refuse to read ungodly books because they think that refusing will make them righteous.

Using the Holiness movement as an example, instead of refusing immodest dress because it violates the Scripture, many in the third generation refrained from immodest apparel as a means of establishing self-righteousness, and eventually they began to adopt immodest apparel by using various justifications and rationalizations. Instead of women wearing their hair long to signify submission to God's plan, the granddaughters often maintained long hair to obtain a degree of holiness: the longer the hair, the greater the righteousness.

Clearly, the third generation can possess a "holiness standard" that is nothing but a warped sense of self-discipline and self-righteousness. This type of piety brings an inconsistent lifestyle. A person can follow a code of conduct, appearing righteous and holy, and yet possess sin of a different category.

For example, individuals may be gluttons in their eating habits and become extremely overweight but consider themselves righteous because they abstain from smoking and drinking. Although attitude problems of jealousy and hatred may develop, people may consider themselves to be righteous because of a godly appearance. Extreme inconsistencies can develop in some cases: someone will participate in open sin such as adultery while refraining from worldly amusements. They may justify unrighteous deeds by adherence to certain codes of conduct of the movement.

Self-centered piety leads to self-righteousness, distorted pharisaic philosophies, and hypocrisy. A mountain of pseudo-piety becomes a monument of inconsistency that leads many in the fourth generation to defect from the movement.

As inconsistencies emerge, people may develop differing means of self-justification. For example, they may place an increasing importance on "feeling" God as a means of assuring themselves that they are godly. By participating in and responding intensely to certain styles of music and by allowing a heavy rhythm to carry them into a different dimension, they may experience an emotional frenzy that is not necessarily of God. This dramatic feeling can lead them to believe that all is well between them and God, when in actuality, they may be participating in open sin that violates God's moral code and leads them far away from God.

With the greater influence on higher education and deeper thought, rationalization can sweep through a movement in the third generation. Individuals may begin to use reason to develop a new type of theology or new approaches to life.

For example, they may rationalize justification as follows: Since a person is justified by faith in Christ, he can live and do as he so desires and remain just (righteous) simply by maintaining his profession of faith. Alternatively, instead of being justified by faith, a person may think that he is justified by his works and that as long as he lives right and does good, he is justified in God's eyes.

Decreasing piety can be rationalized. Statements like the following can infiltrate the movement: "Well, to me . . ."; "That was in the old days, but it's different today."; "In my view, I think . . ."; "I personally see nothing wrong with . . ."; and "We must adapt to this new age." Soon the convictions that the pioneers so strongly embraced slip away and are compromised. Activities once classified as sin are condoned because "the fathers were too narrow and strict."

Accompanying the rationalization of piety, a rationalization of lifestyle occurs, and people live differently from their parents.

Soon salvation itself can be rationalized. Because God is good and merciful, people may say that He will never judge a "good person." Regardless of the Scriptures, people may devise their own theology based on their own thinking.

Many negative factors intermingled together can produce a crystallization effect. As structure grows, the workings of God's Spirit may diminish, and in response, a movement may offer more structure to rectify the problems. The increased structure provides men and women a sense of security, but the process of crystallization only accelerates. Too much structure often limits the work of almighty God, and the cycle continues with people reaching for more structure. The movement peaks, declines, and ultimately dies.

When the third generation yields to the numerous negative characteristics we have described, the fourth generation inherits a denomination but not a true religion. Because the third generation falls from God's truth, God turns away from the fourth generation and focuses on individuals who are hungry for truth.

7

The Sectarian Cycle Summarized

In general terms, then, we can summarize the sectarian cycle as follows. Typically, the first generation of pioneers is God-centered, the second generation is parent-centered, and the third generation is self-centered. The fourth generation then inherits an empty array of rituals and traditions and consequently reverts to the lifestyle prevalent before the movement began.

The first generation of dynamic, revolutionary zealots are characterized by great dedication to God and their infant movement. Because of their zeal, burden, and consecration, the movement flourishes with dynamic growth.

The second generation of adherents are characterized by aspects inherited from their parents. Weary with disorganization, they offer structure to the movement and propel the movement into enhanced growth. Since structure produces increased productivity, and since structure provides people with security, naturally the structure increases. Too much structure often tends to limit the work of God, however. Toward the close of the second generation, structure and rationalization drive the movement to its peak and onto a temporary plateau.

The third-generation adherents, quite defensive in approach, attempt to maintain a declining movement with renewed theology, higher thinking, apologies, and renewed definitions. Structure increases, as well as rationalization. The result of crystallization becomes clearly evident, and the organization that was born to serve the effort and enhance the cause becomes the master. Instead of the organization serving the movement, the movement serves the organization.

Decline and devastation leave to the fourth generation a dead or dying body, which reverts to conditions that existed before the movement began. The stage is set for a new movement to be born and walk through the sectarian cycle.

Of course, this summation of the sectarian cycle contains generalizations and simplifications; it does not necessarily hold true in every respect for every movement and certainly not for every individual within a movement. Moreover, the conversion rate of a movement will directly affect the cycle. The more rapid the growth and numerical conversions experienced by the movement, the slower the sectarian cycle will develop. Converted individuals who enter a second- or third-generation movement provide some first-generation dynamics that restrict the erosion caused by the sectarian cycle. However, these converts tend to gravitate to the established order, ultimately minimizing their first-generation influences.

The Sectarian Cycle

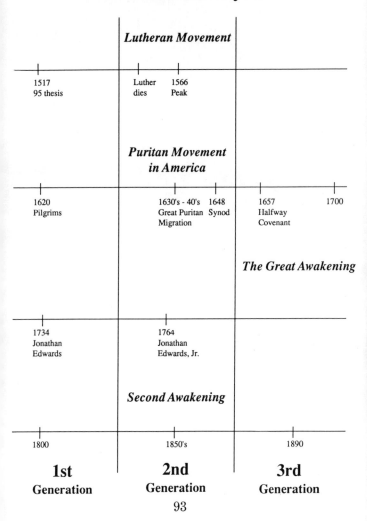

Lutheran Movement

1517 95 thesis	Luther dies	1566 Peak

Puritan Movement in America

1620 Pilgrims	1630's - 40's Great Puritan Migration	1648 Synod	1657 Halfway Covenant	1700

The Great Awakening

1734 Jonathan Edwards	1764 Jonathan Edwards, Jr.

Second Awakening

1800	1850's	1890
1st Generation	**2nd** Generation	**3rd** Generation

The Sectarian Cycle

1st Generation	2nd Generation	3rd Generation
High fervency	Medium fervency	Low fervency
Theological doctrines being defined	Doctrines defined	Little or no tolerance of deviating doctrines
Unstructured	Structure and organization established	Movement serves organization, instead of organization serving movement
Phenomenal kingdom-mindedness	Diminished kingdom-mindedness	Little kingdom-mindedness
Dynamic missionary zeal	Diminished missionary zeal	Little missionary zeal
Dedication to God	Dedication to parents	Dedication to self
Priorities on God	Priorities on parents	Priorities on self
God-centered holiness	Parent-centered holiness	Self-centered holiness

Increased Intellectualism

Structure (Security)
Crystallization

3rd Generation: The Last Generation of Truth

8

Pentecost:
Not a Denomination
But an Experience

The secular student of religion places all
beliefs—whether Buddhism, Shintoism, or Christianity—into a single category and studies them
together. In humanistic studies, such a student
sees all religions as being the same.

Basically, all religions are equivalent—except
apostolic Christianity. Every world religion
follows a similar pattern. Secularly speaking,
every religion begins with a religious man having
a fascinating, tremendous, or mysterious encounter with something he considers to be truth
or deity. Because of the beauty of his experience,

he erects a monument to commemorate this sacred encounter and to establish something that connects heaven with earth.

Resulting from the magnitude and glory of his religious experience, this individual wishes to recreate a similar encounter. He then recalls the events he participated in that led him to his ecstatic or enlightening feeling. If he was kneeling, he again kneels; if he was speaking certain words, he repeats the words. The events of this exercise become emotionally sacred and are taught to others as a ritual.

As the elements of the religious ritual are taught to children and passed from generation to generation, the meaning and purpose of the exercise are often lost. Forgotten are the reasons for kneeling at specific times, repeating specific words at the correct intervals, or other details of the ritual. The skeleton of a ritual remains and is passed from generation to generation, but the meaning of the ritual dissipates.

Even today, many churches participate in meaningless rituals, although they may sing powerful hymns such as:

Years I spent in vanity and pride,
Caring not my Lord was crucified,
Knowing not it was for me he died,
At Calvary.

Mercy there was great and grace was free,
Pardon there was multiplied to me,
There my burdened soul found liberty,
At Calvary.

People can sing hymns such as "Amazing Grace" beautifully in glorious harmony without ever considering the words that they sing. They can utter the words "I love you, Jesus" without genuine, heartfelt meaning. Many times people participate in valid forms of worship only as a meaningless skeleton and ritual.

What is the solution? Abolish the ritual? Eradicate worship? Erase the hymnbook of beautiful songs? No, a thousand times NO! The solution is to rebuild true meaning into the song, word, and worship. We should offer everything we utter or perform with all of our heart!

True Christianity as expressed by the apostolic, Pentecostal doctrine and experience is different from every religion in the world because it never (or should never) merely recreates a past experience. Every encounter, which can occur daily, is a unique experience with God.

Biblical religion may include what scholars call "ritual," but it is ritual with meaning and purpose; moreover every tradition, or ritual, does not merely serve as a memorial of past experiences, but as a pointer toward present and future experiences with God.

Abraham ritualistically pitched his tent, dug a well, and built an altar at each locality where he dwelt. Likewise a child of God worships in every unique experience with God.

When Israel approached the Promised Land the first time, they stopped at Kadesh-Barnea and sent out spies to survey the land of Canaan. Because of unbelief, they returned to the wilderness for forty additional years. The word *Kadesh* in Hebrew means "holy"; to enter the Promised Land, Israel first had to pass the test of consecration. Upon failing, they returned to the wilderness to learn the lesson of trust in God. There they faced the enemy kings Og and Sihon and overcame them. They had to plow up the fallow ground of their hearts and replace empty, ritualistic thinking with true faith and worship.

For example, the Passover became not only a memory of how God delivered the forefathers from Egypt, but also a promise of how God would deliver every Israelite from bondage and give them an inheritance. True consecration was necessary to enter the Promised Land; God never intended for genuine, consistent dedication to degenerate into a meaningless ritual. In God's plan, every ritual must possess purpose and significance.

By consistently maintaining meaning in every ritual and by making every event of worship a significant religious experience without attempting to recreate a prior experience, we can provide the base for consistent growth and counteract the effects of the sectarian cycle. The cycle is not inevitable; people who are sensitive to the almighty God can overcome it by His power.

9

It All Depends on You

Jesus said, "Upon this rock I will build my church" (Matthew 16:18), but the New Testament does not focus primarily on the church as an institution. Romans 13 ordains a place for government and civil instruction, but Paul's inspired writings do not concentrate on this purpose. The Lord God ordained the family unit, but amazingly, something is of even greater importance to the Almighty.

God's primary attention pivots on "you," the individual. Repeatedly, the New Testament declares this message, as we note in the following passages that emphasize "you": "Casting all your care upon him; for he careth for you" (I Peter 5:7); "But the very hairs of your head are all numbered" (Matthew 10:30); "Work out your own salvation with fear and trembling" (Philippians 2:12); "Take heed to yourselves. . . . Watch ye therefore, and pray always, that ye may be accounted worthy" (Luke 21:34, 36).

The human mind tends to focus on organizations, churches, and institutions, but God looks through the mirage of machinery to the person. A family may be falling apart at the seams, but a godly family member can find peace, contentment, and joy in the Lord instead of frustration, because God penetrates the institution to find the individual. Sometimes a church may be tangled in confusion, but God's primary focus will bypass the structure to meet the need of a person. God cares about "you," the individual, more than He cares about any institution, organization, or structure.

It is therefore intriguing to consider how the Scriptures develop the emphasis on "you." God's chief consideration in His relationship to people is based upon their attitude. Our relationship to God is not predicated upon position, abilities, heritage, or talents. From Adam until now, when godly, blessed men and women turned from God to wickedness, they did not escape God's judgment. Conversely, when wicked people, such as the Ninevites, repented and humbly confessed their sins to God and requested mercy, He gently expressed His lovingkindness to them. A proper attitude toward God serves as the foundation for healthy human-divine relationships. As Peter declared, "God resisteth the proud, and giveth grace to the humble" (I Peter 5:5).

Although the sectarian cycle generally operates over three generations, persons within a movement may escape the cyclic tendencies. Regardless of a movement's generational trends, because God's focus is directed to "you," He still finds hungry individuals and extends to them benefits, while turning from those who have alienated themselves from godly principles.

For example, God denied the eldest son's blessing to Esau, the first-born of Isaac and a third-generation member of the "patriarchal movement." While he was physically famished, Esau considered his birthright worthless. Selling his birthright to his younger brother, he visibly displayed his carnal priorities, and God ultimately granted the blessing to Jacob. He passed over the elder son and blessed the younger son. Apparently, God looks at a person's attitude rather than his position, credentials, or heritage.

Numerous times this type of story is reiterated, but ultimately each drama depicts God's relationship to humanity. When Israel turned to idolatry, God focused His affection and blessings upon another. In Paul's terminology, God cut off the old branch and grafted in a new branch, the Gentile church.

The three young Hebrew men in Babylonian captivity were faithful to godly principles and caused the grand structure of the Babylonian empire to bow humbly to their God. God pierced a massive, established bureaucracy to salvage three precious individuals. He passed through a mighty organization to save what was more important to Him—not a movement, but people.

Repeatedly Jesus bypassed pharisaical traditions to deliver, heal, or save just one. "You" is the New Testament emphasis, and Jesus beautifully illustrated this principle by the parable of the one lost sheep: the shepherd left the secure sheepfold to provide love and safety to the singular and isolated.

While a movement is shifting toward cyclic trends, God continues to bless genuinely hungry, desirous souls. Third-generation believers who have a fervent desire for the things of God may obtain a first- or second-generation level of dedication, thus passing on to their children either second- or third-generation tendencies rather than fourth.

Organizations or institutions cannot escape the harsh trends of the sectarian cycle merely by corporate action. Only individuals, in isolated closets of prayer, can successfully make an impact on themselves and their families. When adequate and sufficient numbers of persons within their private circles unselfishly devote to God a lifestyle of complete consecration, then a movement may reverse the generational tendencies and see an increase of life, vibrancy, and fervency. It all depends on "you."

10

A Third Generation with a First-Generation Experience

For the sad, degenerating process by which movements experience the sectarian cycle, God provides a beautiful remedy: every generation may obtain a first-generation experience. Since true believers are the unique group who can encounter a fresh experience daily, no reason or excuse should hinder any hungry person from possessing a God-centered walk.

Today, more than any other age, we need genuine dedication to God by seeking first the

kingdom of God and His righteousness. Material-
ism, ambitions, and goals must take second place
to God almighty. Not only must Jesus reign, but
we need to dedicate ourselves to His cause and
spend ourselves for His purpose. We must rebuke
mediocrity, hypocrisy, apathy, and lethargy and
march to the forefront as staunch soldiers for the
King. The Master calls for more praying and less
playing, more commitment and less complaining,
more consecration and less relaxation, more
dedication!

It is imperative today that the church possess
a God-centered piety. We need to comprehend that
our righteousness is only as filthy rags in His sight,
and nothing we can accomplish will make us holy.
Only God can grant remission of sins, righteousness, and a holy nature.

However, a sanctified individual should live in
this God-given holiness by refraining from physical, mental, emotional, or spiritual defilement and
by consecrating himself continually to God. God's
mandate is plain: "Be ye holy; for I am holy." In
other words, by His grace we can and must stay
cleansed.

Although many people today passively occupy
their place in the church house, caring nothing
about lost neighbors and friends and displaying
their lack of dedication, some will rise above this
mediocre attitude and maintain a God-centered

dedication, which always produces a dynamic missionary zeal. With a deep consecration, they will feel the heartbeat of Jesus Christ: "The Son of man is come to seek and to save that which was lost" (Luke 19:10). Their constant craving to see the lost saved—to see individuals truly born again of water and of the Spirit—motivates the deeply dedicated to share their witness with neighbors, relatives, and friends. Without relaxing to allow others to assume their responsibility, they are determined to fulfill their personal commission to go and teach all nations.

Today is the time for the church to push aside all complacency and maintain the pioneer attitude of continually desiring for personal spiritual growth. Never becoming satisfied with the status quo in our spiritual walk, we must constantly nurture a hunger for more and more of Jesus.

Let us offer sincere worship and praise unto God. Let every "ritual" exalt Jesus Christ. Let every action possess biblical significance. Let everything we do "in word or deed" be done in the name of Jesus (Colossians 3:17).

The sectarian cycle presently challenges the Oneness Pentecostal movement with intimidating lessons from history. Its harsh trends glare at the People of the Name. Given the tendencies of self-centeredness, rationalization, and rigidity of organization and theology that promote the sectarian cycle, the third generation of the Oneness Pentecostal movement faces its greatest challenge and responsibility.

If we yield apathetically to the historical trends of religious movements, we will grant to fourth-generation believers a devastated, diluted, impotent body that is unable to save, heal, or deliver. If parents become dedicated primarily to themselves, they will hopelessly offer their children a "form of godliness" possessing no power (II Timothy 3:5).

The only viable option for true survival demands selfless dedication and complete consecration to God. We must wholeheartedly embrace the evangelism of others, true humility, sacrificial living, and godly righteousness. We will only preserve our heritage by vigorously attacking and defeating the trends of the sectarian cycle. The third generation must possess a first-generation lifestyle and experience.

The Oneness Pentecostal movement holds great potential for overcoming the sectarian cycle we have described. Let us determine that, despite adversity and persecution, the third generation of the Oneness Pentecostal movement shall emerge from the battle with history unscathed and undefeated, embracing the identity of Jesus Christ and the power of His name. Let it never be declared of this movement that their third generation was their last generation of truth. The promise of the Lord Jesus Christ Himself proclaims the inexhaustible potential available to the third generation of the Oneness Pentecostal movement: "I know thy works: behold, I have set before thee an open door, and no man can shut it: for thou hast a little strength, and hast kept my word, and hast not denied my name" (Revelation 3:8).

NOTES

[1]Interview with Reverend E. L. Holley, August 19, 1989. The date of the Methodist Episcopal Church South meeting was either 1864 or 1865.

[2]Richard B. Wilke, *And Are We Yet Alive* (Nashville: Abingdon Press, 1987), p. 9.

[3]Sydney E. Ahlstrom, *A Religious History of the American People* (Binghampton, N.Y.: Vail-Ballou Press, Inc., 1972), p. 29.

[4]L. Christiani, *L'Eglise a l'Epoque du Concile de Trente*, ed. A. Flinche and V. Martin (Paris, 1948), p. 247. Translated by S. E. Ahlstrom.

[5]Kenneth Scott Latourette, *A History of Christianity: Reformation to the Present* (New York: Harper and Row Publishers, 1975), vol. 2, p. 707.

[6]Ahlstrom, p. 245.

[7]Martin E. Marty, "Lutheranism," *Americana Encyclopedia* 1972, vol 17, p. 868.

[8]Ibid., p. 867.

[9]Ahlstrom, p. 236.

[10]John McClintock and James Strong, "Pietism," *Cyclopedia of Biblical, Theological, and Ecclesiastical Literature* (Grand Rapids: Baker Book House, 1981), vol. 8, p. 193.

[11]Vergilius Ferm (ed.), "Neo-Lutheranism," *An Encyclopedia of Religion* (N.Y.: Philosophical Library, 1945), p. 524.

[12]Henry H. Halley, *Halley's Bible Handbook* (Grand Rapids: Zondervan Publishing House, 1965), p. 791.

[13]John R. H. Moorman, *A History of the Church in England* (New York: Morehouse-Barlow, 1959), pp. 168-69.

[14]George F. Willison, *Saints and Strangers* (New York: Reynal and Hitchcock, 1964), pp. 29-30.

[15]George M. Trevelyan, *England Under the Stuarts,* 16th ed. (London: Methuen and Co., 1933), pp. 60-71.

[16]Ahlstrom, p. 91.

[17]Latourette, pp. 819-20.

[18]Ahlstrom, pp. 185-87. Information in this and the following three paragraphs discussing Jamestown was obtained from this source.

[19]Ibid., p. 186.

[20]Willison, pp. 165-68.

[21]Ibid.

[22]Anson P. Atterbury, "The Pilgrims," a paper read at a meeting of the Colonial Dames of the State of New York, January 4, 1920 (the tercentenary year of the landing of the Pilgrim Fathers), printed by request of the Board of Managers, p. 11.

[23]Willison, pp. 165-68.

[24]Ahlstrom, pp. 106, 141-42.

[25]Williston Walker, *The Creeds and Platforms of Congregationalism* (Boston: Pilgrim Press, 1960), p. 116.

[26]Ahlstrom, p. 147.

[27]Ibid., p. 145.

[28]Willison, p. 28.

[29]Ahlstrom, p. 146-47.

[30]Ibid., p. 124.

[31]Ibid., p. 151. All five problems are mentioned.

[32]Ibid., p. 158.

[33]Ibid., pp. 158-59.

[34]Ibid., pp. 160, 164.

[35]*Magnalia Christi Americana,* (Hartford edition, 1820), vol. 1, p. 59.

[36]Ahlstrom, p. 282.

[37]Edwin Scott Gaustad, *The Great Awakening in New England* (New York: Harper and Row, 1962). p. 20.

[38]Ahlstrom, p. 284.

[39]Ibid., p. 285.

[40]Ibid., p. 287.

[41]Paul Johnson, *A History of Christianity* (New York: Atheneum, 1977), p. 366.

[42]Herbert W. Schneider, *The Puritan Mind,* (Ann Arbor: University of Michigan Press, 1958), p. 208.

[43]Bennet Tyler, *New England Revivals . . . from Narratives First Published in the Connecticut Evangelical Magazine* (Boston, 1846), p. 59.

[44]Vernon L. Parrington, *Main Currents in American Thought* (New York: Harcourt, Brace & Co., 1927), vol. 1, pp. 158, 162-63.

[45]Ahlstrom, p. 414.

[46]Quoted in Charles Roy Keller, *The Second Great Awakening in Connecticut* (New Haven, Yale University Press, 1942), pp. 37-38.

[47]Ahlstrom, p. 433.

[48]Barton W. Stone, "A Short History of the Life of Barton W. Stone Written by Himself," in *Voices from Cane Ridge,* ed. Rhodes Thompson, facsimile ed. (St. Louis: Bethany Press, 1954), p. 68.

[49]Ibid., pp. 69-72.

[50]Ahlstrom, pp. 426-28. Information in this and the preceding three paragraphs discussing the results of the Second Awakening was obtained from this source.

[51]William W. Sweet, *Religion in the Development of American Culture, 1765-1840* (New York: Charles Scribner's Sons, 1952) p. 119.

[52]Ahlstrom, p. 437.

[53]Ibid., p. 732.

[54]Ibid., pp. 718-19.

[55]Walter A. Elwell (ed), *Evangelical Dictionary of Theology* (Grand Rapids: Baker Book House, 1984), p. 517.

[56]John L. Sherrill, *They Speak with Other Tongues* (Old Tappan, N.J.: Fleming H. Revell Company, 1964), pp. 38-39.

[57]Ahlstrom, pp. 820-21.

[58]Ibid.

[59]Interview by E. S. Caldwell, "The Assemblies Through the Eyes of C. M. Ward," *Charisma,* August 1989, pp. 46-47.

[60]Ahlstrom, p. 822.

[61]Edward E. Plowman, "The Assemblies of God: Seventy-five Years of Faith, Outreach and Growth," *Charisma,* August 1989, p. 41.

[62]Interview with Nola Willhoite, November 25, 1988. Mrs. Willhoite, at age nine, was baptized in Jesus' name at this revival.

[63]Interview with Reverend N. A. Urshan, August 14, 1989. N. A. Urshan is the son of A. D. Urshan.

[64]Ahlstrom, p. 821.

[65]"United Pentecostal Church," *The New Enclopaedia Britannica,* 1985, vol. 12, p. 150.

[66]Interview with Reverend James Kilgore, August 29, 1989. Reverend Kilgore is the son of C. P. Kilgore.

[67]Interview with Reverend R. C. Wise, November 24, 1988. Reverend Wise served as pastor of the church mentioned.

Bibliography

Ahlstrom, Sydney E. *A Religious History of the American People.* Binghampton, N.Y.: Vail-Ballou Press, Inc., 1972.

Atterbury, Anson P. "The Pilgrims." A paper read at a meeting of the Colonial Dames of the State of New York, January 4, 1920. Printed by request of the Board of Managers.

Caldwell, E. S. "The Assemblies Through the Eyes of C. M. Ward." *Charisma,* August 1989, pp. 46-47.

Christiani, L. *L'Eglise a l'Epoque du Concile de Trente.* Flinche, A. and Martin, V. (ed.). Paris: 1948. Translated by S. E. Ahlstrom.

Elwell, Walter A. (ed.). *Evangelical Dictionary of Theology.* Grand Rapids: Baker Book House, 1984.

Fern, Vergilius (ed.). "Neo-Lutheranism," *An Encyclopedia of Religion.* New York: Philosophical Library, 1945.

Gaustad, Edwin Scott. *The Great Awakening in New England.* New York: Harper and Row, 1962.

Halley, Henry H. *Halley's Bible Handbook.* Grand Rapids: Zondervan, 1965.

Holley, E. L. Interview August 19, 1989.

Johnson, Paul. *A History of Christianity.* New York: Atheneum, 1977.

Keller, Charles Roy. *The Second Great Awakening in Connecticut*. New Haven; Yale University Press, 1942.

Kilgore, James. Interview August 29, 1989.

Latourette, Kenneth Scott. *A History of Christianity: Reformation to the Present,* 3 vols. New York: Harper and Row, 1975.

Magnalia Christi Americana, 2 vols. Hartford Edition, 1820.

Marty, Martin E. "Lutheranism," *Americana Encyclopedia* 1972, vol 17.

McClintock, John and Strong, James. "Pietism," *Cyclopedia of Biblical, Theological, and Ecclesiastical Literature*. Grand Rapids: Baker Book House, 1981.

Moorman, John R. H. *A History of the Church in England*. New York: Morehouse-Barlow, 1959.

Parrington, Vernon L. *Main Currents in American Thought*. New York: Harcourt, Brace & Co., 1927.

Plowman, Edward E. "The Assemblies of God: Seventy-five Years of Faith, Outreach and Growth." *Charisma,* August 1989, p. 41.

Schneider, Herbert W. *The Puritan Mind*. Ann Arbor: University of Michigan Press, 1958.

Sherrill, John L. *They Speak with Other Tongues*. Old Tappan, New Jersey: Fleming H. Revell, 1964.

Stone, Barton W. "A Short History of the Life

of Barton W. Stone Written by Himself," *Voices from Cane Ridge,* Thompson, Rhodes (ed.) facsimile ed. St. Louis: Bethany Press, 1954.

Sweet, William W. *Religion in the Development of American Culture, 1765-1840.* New York: Charles Scribner's Sons, 1952.

Trevelyan, George M. *England Under the Stuarts,* 16th ed. London: Methuen and Co., 1933.

Tyler, Bennet. *New England Revivals . . . from Narratives First Published in the Connecticut Evangelical Magazine.* Boston, 1846.

"United Pentecostal Church," *The New Encyclopaedia Britannica.* Chicago: William Benton, 1985.

Urshan, N. A. Interview August 14, 1989.

Walker, Williston. *The Creeds and Platforms of Congregationalism.* Boston: Pilgrim Press, 1960.

Willhoite, Nola. Interview November 25, 1988.

Willison, George F. *Saints and Strangers.* New York: Reynal and Hitchcock, 1964.

Wilke, Richard B. *And Are We Yet Alive.* Nashville: Abingdon Press, 1987.

Wise, R. C. Interview November 24, 1988.

About the Author

With his lovely wife, Pam, at his side, Reverend Daniel L. Butler has faithfully ministered before the Lord within the circle of the United Pentecostal Church International for over ten years. Raised as a third-generation Oneness Pentecostal, he conscientiously serves his God, dedicated to the cause inherited from God-fearing grandparents.

Born and raised in central Indiana, upon high school graduation he aggressively pursued a profession in medicine. Upon his fulfilling the necessary requirements for a major in Biology and minors in Chemistry and Religious Studies, Purdue University conferred upon him the Bachelor of Science degree. Instead of enrolling in medical school, however, he decided to follow other interests and attended Jackson College of Ministries in Jackson, Mississippi.

In ministerial service, Dan and his family have served as assistant pastor and school principal in Irving, Texas, evangelized from church to church, and pastored a congregation in Birmingham, Alabama. He has founded two Christian parochial schools and served as the Alabama District youth president. Presently Dan serves as the Director of Prison Ministry and the General Home Missions Secretary of the United Pentecostal Church International in Hazelwood, Missouri. His responsibilities take him across North America preaching, teaching, and training on local, district, and national levels.

In 1983, the Lord blessed Dan and Pam with their cherished son, Dane.